HAL•LEONARD
INSTRUMENTAL
PLAY-ALONG

# FLUTE

# STEPHEN SONDHEIM BROADWAY SOLOS

# CONTENTS

THE CD IS PLAYABLE ON ANY CD PLAYER, AND IS ALSO ENHANCED SO MAC AND PC USERS CAN ADJUST THE RECORDING TO ANY TEMPO WITHOUT CHANGING THE PITCH.

ISBN 978-1-4234-7277-3

RILTING MUSIC, INC.

EXCLUSIVELY DISTRIBUTED BY

HAL•LEONARD®
CORPORATION

7777 W. BLUEMOUND RD. P.O. BOX 13819 MILWAUKEE, WI 53213

Visit Hal Leonard Online at
**www.halleonard.com**

# ANYONE CAN WHISTLE

from ANYONE CAN WHISTLE

Words and Music by
STEPHEN SONDHEIM

FLUTE

# BEING ALIVE

from COMPANY

Music and Lyrics by
STEPHEN SONDHEIM

**FLUTE**

# BROADWAY BABY

### from FOLLIES

 **5/6**

**FLUTE**

Music and Lyrics by
STEPHEN SONDHEIM

# CHILDREN WILL LISTEN

from INTO THE WOODS

**7/8**

**FLUTE**

Words and Music by
STEPHEN SONDHEIM

# COMEDY TONIGHT
from A FUNNY THING HAPPENED ON THE WAY TO THE FORUM

Words and Music by
STEPHEN SONDHEIM

**FLUTE**

# GOOD THING GOING

from MERRILY WE ROLL ALONG

 **11/12**

**FLUTE**

Words and Music by
STEPHEN SONDHEIM

# JOHANNA
from SWEENEY TODD

13/14

**FLUTE**

Words and Music by
STEPHEN SONDHEIM

# LOSING MY MIND

from FOLLIES

Music and Lyrics by
STEPHEN SONDHEIM

# NOT A DAY GOES BY

from MERRILY WE ROLL ALONG

**17/18**

**FLUTE**

Words and Music by
STEPHEN SONDHEIM

# NOT WHILE I'M AROUND

from SWEENEY TODD

Words and Music by
STEPHEN SONDHEIM

FLUTE

# OLD FRIENDS
## from MERRILY WE ROLL ALONG

Words and Music by
STEPHEN SONDHEIM

FLUTE

# PRETTY WOMEN

from SWEENEY TODD

Words and Music by
STEPHEN SONDHEIM

FLUTE

# SEND IN THE CLOWNS
## from the Musical A LITTLE NIGHT MUSIC

Words and Music by
STEPHEN SONDHEIM

FLUTE

# SUNDAY

### from SUNDAY IN THE PARK WITH GEORGE

FLUTE

Words and Music by
STEPHEN SONDHEIM